MAGYAR NAMES
for
Hungarian Dogs

Edited by Jackie Isabell

Cover Design by Bob Groves

DENLINGER'S PUBLISHERS, LTD.
Box 76, Fairfax, Virginia 22030

Acknowledgments

I wish to express my sincere appreciation and thanks to all who have given so freely of their time, photographs, and untiring efforts to help make this book a valuable asset to all who profess an interest and love for the Hungarian breeds.

Photographs: Canadian Kennel Club; Christophe Carrier, France; Claudie Ducret, France; Ed Flesh, California; Bonnie and Mark Goodwein, California; James and Patsy Jones, California; Anna Marie Llewellyn, Ohio; David Powers, California; Andrew Rohringer, California; Lorna E. Spangenberg, Oregon; Nicole Thillier, France; Corrine Trainel, France; and David Zanavich, California.

Assistance with translations and correspondence: Helene Gourland-Hamilton, California; Ildiko Samay, California.

Foreign connection with the Hungarian Kennel Club: Denise Hamilton (*Los Angeles Times* staff writer), California.

Library of Congress Cataloging-in-Publication Data

Zerebko, Irene
    Magyar names for Hungarian dogs / by Irene
Zerebko ; edited by Jackie Isabell.
      p. cm.
    ISBN 0-87714-154-1
    1. Dogs—Names. 2. Names, Hungarian. 3. Dog
breeds—Hungary.
    I. Isabell, Jackie. II. Title.
    SF429.3.Z46 1993
    636.7—dc20
                                91-29408

International Standard Book Number: 0-87714-154-1

Dedication

Remembering my father; who loved a good dog and a challenge.

Puli. Sketch by Sylvia S. Owen, goddaughter of John Singer Sergent. Courtesy of David Powers and Ed Flesh, Sylmar, California.

Mudi. Courtesy of the Canadian Kennel Club.

Foreword

This book does not treat in more than a general way the details of the origin and characteristics of the various Hungarian breeds.

Among the host of dog lovers through the ages, one finds a common denominator—the search for a name that best befits that "special" dog and which subtly embodies it with some of its owner's personality and imagination, drawn from fiction, fancy, or fantasy. Originally, the Magyars referred to dogs by names descriptive of their work rather than by type or variety. Undoubtedly, favored dogs were given names denoting their valor, thus distinguishing them from lesser hounds and forming the basis of closer bonds with their masters.

At first glance, the reader might feel that the Hungarian language will be difficult to use; however, if time is spent on "The Hungarian Language" and "The Hungarian Alphabet and Pronunciation Guide" sections, it will soon become easy to sound out the words. Diacritical marks may be used at the discretion of the reader but should not be obligatory for registration purposes.

Several examples follow to give the reader an idea of how best to utilize the book in compiling names in the vernacular:

- Halas Fehér Erika (Halas White Heather) uses words from the lists on "Geographic Areas of Interest," "Colors in AKC Standards," and "Flowers, Trees, and Shrubs"

- Kossuth is a name from the section on "Hungarians Who Influenced History and Culture"

- Réz Kacér (Copper Coquette) combines words from "Metals and Precious Jewels" and "General Alphabetic Listing"

The reader is offered a myriad of short but phonetically pleasing and unique words, names, places, and other subjects of interest from which to draw unusual and original affixes and names.

I.H.Z.

Pulik. Eng. Imp. Amer. Ch. Borgvaale Napoleon Brandy,

Amer. Ch. Gitana Jerez, and Mex., & Amer. Ch. Temblor Celebrity Sweepstakes.

Owned by David Powers and Ed Flesh, Sylmar, California.

Contents

*Hungarian stamps depicting the four most popular breeds—Puli, Vizsla,
Kuvasz, and Komondor (puppy).*

Dogs of Hungarian Origin

Because of its geographical location, making it somewhat of an ecological bridge across Europe, and variable terrain, Hungary has been able to produce and preserve a variety of dog breeds found nowhere else in the world. The mountainous regions gave rise to sheepherding and guard dogs with thick coats, which protected them from attacking wolves, while the vast plains were the fountainhead of the Hungarian coursing and hunting breeds.

Sheepherding Dogs

The first reference to a Puli appears in Hungarian literature in 1751; the first description of the Hungarian sheepdog dates back to 1767 by Páriz-Pápai, a doctor of medicine and compiler of dictionaries. In the ancient Dravidian language, the word *Puli* was applied to a specific method of herd driving. Originally, the term *Pulik* (plural of Puli) referred to all types of Hungarian sheepherding dogs; Pulik were multicolored dogs of varying size, depending on the needs of the herdsmen, who deemed herding instincts and willingness to work more important than outward appearance, size, or color.

At the beginning of the twentieth century when controlled breeding began, zoologists—with the help of Dr. Emile Raitsits, a leading Hungarian expert on animal breeding—classified the Puli and the Pumi as individual breeds, and carefully planned selective breeding for the past fifty years has been directed toward eliminating all overlapping characteristics of the Puli and the Pumi. They also identified a third type of sheepherding dog that Mr. Dezso Fényesi, an advocate of selective breeding, called *Mudi*.

Puli. Today's Pulik emerged as medium-sized, vigorous, alert, affectionate dogs whose herding instincts have been preserved. They are devoted, home loving, and good guard dogs without aggressiveness.

The preferred color is black, though whites have increased in number and popularity during the 1980s. Various shades of gray are also acceptable. The different types of coat depend on hair structure and mode of grooming. The dogs range from 40 to 44 cm (17–19 inches) in height, and the bitches from 37 to 41 cm (16–18 inches).

9

Pumi. The active, lively, and energetic Pumi are adaptable to working with sheep, cattle, and pigs. Dr. Emile Raitsits, a professor of veterinary medicine and leading Hungarian expert on animal breeding, referred to the *Pumi* as "sheep dog terrier." About the size of a Fox Terrier, Pumi are audacious drovers, able to handle the most obstinate cattle, and make excellent guardians. The terrier qualities have endowed the breed with great intelligence, a passion for rat hunting, and a keen sense of smell. They are assertive and inclined to be noisy.

Any coat color is acceptable as long as it is solid. The Pumi are described as herding terriers with medium-long coats. The coat is a fifty-fifty ratio of rough topcoat and a finer undercoat that does not mat or cord. The size ranges from 35 to 44 cm (13-17 inches), with little difference between dogs and bitches.

Mudi. Since they are not as yet closely bred, Mudi have different regional varieties, and they are virtually unknown outside Hungary. However, all have lively temperaments and great herding and hunting ability. Lively and quick, the Mudi is easy to maintain and makes an excellent house pet.

Mudi can be black, white, particolored, or *pepita*—an evenly distributed mixture of colors that is a peculiarity of the breed. The coat can be wavy or curly. Dogs and bitches are similar in size, and weight ranges from 8 to 13 kg (about 17-19 pounds).

Sheep-Guarding Dogs

When Magyar tribes entered Hungary in the ninth century, they brought flocks of sheep known as *Racka* and large aggressive guard dogs, possibly originating in Tibet. The sheep, which were of large size with curly wool and an aura of proud carriage rather than typical sheepishness, had a strange affinity to the dogs. The Magyars used these dogs not only to guard the flocks from predators but also in warfare.

Komondor. The largest of the Hungarian breeds, the Komondor is characterized by an unusual appearance and commanding manner. Loyal and with a charming disposition, Komondorok make noble companions, distrustful of strangers. This is not, however, a breed for an inexperienced or novice pet owner, and they must be treated with respect.

Being a very positive breed with a strong personality, the Komondor was perfect for guarding the large and assertive Racka, and historians believe that the Komondor was instrumental in eradicating the wolf from Hungary. The Komondor is highly prized by shepherd masters, and in the Hortagy region where they are most likely to be seen, breeding is conducted with the greatest conservation, care, and selection.

10

The earliest written record of the word *Komondor* is dated 1544. In 1673, Amos Comenius wrote in ancient Hungarian, *"Komondoroc oerzic a csordat,"* meaning "Komondorok guard the herd." In his *Natural History,* Ferenc Pethe calls the Komondor "leader of the dogs."

There are several theories on the origin of the name. It is possible that *Ku (Ku-mondor)*—derived from the ancient Sumerian word *ku-dda*—was translated into modern Hungarian as *kutya,* meaning dog. Some linguists claim that the name, derived from the French *Commondeur* or the Italian *Cane Commondore,* means leader or leader dog.

White is the only acceptable color because it delineates the dogs from the predators. The Komondor's coat needs attention from an early age, or it will form a solid armorlike mat. The best-known coat formations are as follows: matted hair, ribbons, wide ribbons, tassels, and plain cords. The height for dogs is about 80 cm (25 inches) and afor bitches about 70 cm (23½ inches).

Kuvasz. Probably the best-known of all Hungarian dogs, the Kuvasz is characterized by a beautiful, expressive head; the breed is large but well balanced, with remarkable agility. They are highly intelligent, devoted, and gentle, with a great inclination to guard children and a natural aversion to strangers as well as unfailing courage and an eagerness to attack. Kuvasz take their duties seriously and must never be dealt with harshly lest they become difficult to manage.

Many believe the Kuvasz originated in Turkey—*Kuvasz* means "guardian of the nobles" in Turkish. Recent research, however, suggests that the breed originated in the region of ancient Sumer about 3500 B.C. The first mention of the Kuvasz as an individual breed dates back to the 1600s. The first illustrations of Kuvasz and Komondor as separate breeds are found in Ferenc Pethe's *Natural History.* Friedrich Treitschke (1776-1842), a natural scientist, refers to the Kuvasz as *hirsutus,* meaning hairy.

King Mátyás Corvinus (The Just), who reigned during the fifteenth century, always had a Kuvasz at his side wherever he went. He kept a large kennel at the palace, placing more trust in his dogs than in his guards. It was mainly due to his efforts that the breed not only survived but also improved and flourished.

As with the Komondor, white is the only acceptable color. One of the breed's best features is a heavy thick coat that never mats or cords. The height for dogs is about 71-75 cm (28-29½ inches)and for bitches about 66-70 cm (26-27½ inches).

Counterparts of the Kuvasz, developed for the same type of work, can be found all over the world under a variety of names and colors.

Hunting Dogs

Although all dogs possess basic hunting instincts, specific and distinct characteristics have been developed in hunting breeds to correspond with need, terrain, weather, and indigenous game. The Hungarian hunting breeds fall into three distinct groups: (a) Vizsla (smooth and wirehaired)—a versatile searching, pointing, and retrieving gundog; Agár (greyhound)—a swift dog to bring down small and large game; and Kopó (Transylvanian Hound)—for hunting on horseback.

Vizsla (smooth). Today's Vizsla is a good-natured dog, adept at working on land as well as in water and trainable for any hunting task that might be required, making it ideal for the professional sportsman. It is elegant, clean, and companionable as well as a devoted house dog.

The Vizsla was already known during the Arpád Dynasty (ninth through fourteenth centuries). A 1510 document shows that the Vizsla was highly prized to flush quail when bird hunting was carried out by means of nets. It is surmised that the color was developed by crossbreeding with yellow Turkish pointing dogs, and the name originated from the Turkish word *seek*.

Vizsla (wirehaired). The wirehaired variety, which is not well-known outside its homeland, appeared approximately forty years ago as a result of spontaneous mutation and also due to crossbreeding with wirehaired German pointers. Although in most respects exactly like the smooth-coated Vizsla, the wirehair is a bit coarser in structure, being bred for serious work and retrieval in icy waters. It is highly intelligent, with a well-balanced temperament and a superb nose, but it does not make a good house pet.

Agár. In some European countries, today's Agár can be found in the field, on the racetrack, and in the show ring. The breed is hardy, alert, and watchful, with great stamina and adaptability to climatic changes and makes a quiet, faithful companion in the home.

When Magyar tribes crossed the mountains into the Carpathian Basin during the ninth century, they brought with them not only herding and guard dogs but also the Agár's ancestor—a swift greyhound-type dog, capable of bringing down game on the run. They used the Agár to course the big hare that frequents the Hungarian *Puszta* (plain), often retrieving the kill, as well as running down roe deer, red deer, and even wolf. Several assumptions have been made as to the breed's origin since drawings of greyhound-type dogs have been found in Babylonian, Assyrian, Roman, and Egyptian ruins.

During the Middle Ages, the Agár became the favorite of nobility not only because of its elegance but also because hunting with greyhounds was the fashion of the day. Many such hunts were depicted on medieval tapestries.

In the late nineteenth century, English Greyhounds were brought into Hungary in order to increase the Agár's speed and elegance. Eventually, it became apparent that many of the breed's original characteristics were being dissipated. Especially affected were the coat texture and contour, which became too refined. Great effort has been made to restore the Agár to its ancestral type.

All color variations are acceptable. The dogs average 63 cm (25 inches) and the bitches 60 cm (24 inches) in height.

Kopó (Transylvanian Hound). Seldom seen outside Hungary, the Kopó is known for its benevolent attitude, bravery, and perseverance. It is fiercely protective and loyal to its owner. Great care is being taken to preserve the original characteristics of the breed.

The Kopó is not a pack hunter. It is excellent at beating and trailing, giving tongue in pursuit, and has been known to bay a deer to a standstill. The Kopó is dauntless but so tractable that it can be trained to retrieve. The larger-type Kopó is used to hunt game such as boar, lynx, and so forth for which the breed bears a passionate hatred; the smaller-type—thought to be extinct—was used to hunt hare and fox.

Two varieties of beagle-type dog were found in the Carpathian Basin. There are no historic documents to indicate if these were indigenous or were the legacy of Huns and Avars passing through before the Magyars. Dog bones found in excavations attest to the fact that beagle-type dogs existed in the Carpathian Basin at the time of the Great Migration. The Kopó's value to hunters was so legendary that, as Diezel-Mika writes in his book *Hunting Dogs,* it was not out of the ordinary to exchange a three-year-old Carpathian colt for a good dog.

During the tenth through sixteenth centuries, the breeds were referred to as the Pannon Kopó; during the Middle Ages as the Hungarian Kopó; and later as the Black Hungarian Kopó. Today it is known as the Kopó or the Transylvanian Hound, where it flourished and adapted to the environment and to the diversified indigenous game found in the heavily wooded districts.

The larger or longer-legged variety has a coarser, denser coat that is mostly black, with tan on the chest and legs and sometimes a touch of white. The smaller or shorter-legged variety has a finer reddish coat, lightening at the chest and legs; white spots may occur, and the muzzle may be "smoky." The height is 55–65 cm (21–25½ inches) for the larger variety and 30–35 cm (17½–20 inches) for the smaller variety.

13

Komondor. Int., Mex., & Amer. Ch. Nemessanyi Attila FCM. Owned by Andrew Rohringer, Alta Loma, California (pictured with owner).

Evolution of the Hungarian Language

Being of the Finno-Ugrian language, Hungarian—also called Magyar—does not belong to the Indo-European language group but rather to the one known as Ural-Altaic.

- *Ural-Altaic languages:* Samoïedic, Ugrian, Turkish, Mongolian, Manchu
- *Finno-Ugrian people:* Finnish, Cheremis, Sirenian, Hungarian, Vogul, Estonian, Mordvinian, Votiak, Ostiak

Lapps, though ethnically different, were somewhat influenced by the Finnish language.

The modern Hungarian alphabet uses Latin characters, with a total of forty letters—fourteen vowels and twenty-six consonants. During its first millenium, Hungarian was written in a script similar to the Turkic, but in the eleventh-century A.D., the Latin alphabet was introduced and adopted in a modified form.

The nineteenth-century German linguist Jacob Grimm advocated that the Hungarian language be made the language of diplomacy since it is easy to learn as far as grammar and pronunciation are concerned. The Hungarian vocabulary has borrowed words from other languages such as Turkic, Slavic, and German.

When spoken, the Hungarian language is very melodious. Feelings and thoughts are expressed with nuances and modulations of voice or fluctuations in the phrase or sentence. In speaking, questions are indicated by voice inflection alone. There is no declension nor grammatical gender in Magyar. Quantity is enough to show plurality—that is, "two man sits" rather than "two men are sitting."

Very few Magyar words of more than one syllable cannot be broken down into small components, each with a specific meaning.

Diacritical marks indicate modifications of vowel sounds not found in the Latin Alphabet. In the section on "The Hungarian Alphabet and Pronunciation Guide," the diacritical marks should assist the reader by facilitating correct pronunciation. However, diacritical marks have been purposely omitted in the section on "Hungarians Who Influenced History and Culture," since many have migrated to the United States and have modified pronunciation of their names to conform with American style of speech.

Puli (corded). Int., Mes., & Amer. Ch. & Ch. of Americas Temblo Chain Reaction. Owned by David Powers and Ed Flesh, Sylmar, California.

The Hungarian Alphabet and Pronunciation Guide

In the listings that follow, in order to facilitate pronunciation for the reader, the auther decided to forego the alphabetic sounds and substituted "sounds like" letters to formulate Hungarian words. Since many same letters in the Hungarian alphabet have slight sound variations due to diacritical marks, the author used the closest possible combinations to produce the needed sound. To get the best results, the reader should run together the phonetics, thus producing the most correct pronunciation.

Since the Magyar language does not have words beginning with the letters *q, w, x,* and *y,* the latter have been omitted from all listings.

Letter	Sounds Like	As in
a	ah	dart, mart, heart
á	auh	bought, small
b	beh	beam, boy, beg
c	ts	its, bits, wits
cs	ch	church, birch
d	deh	dog, drab, did
dz	dz	Windsor
dzs	djeh	John, joke, July
e	eh	get, ember, where
é	ey	hay, may, cake
f	ef	fire, firm, fill
g	geh	gallon, go, grief
gy	gyew	dew, few
h	heh	ham, hold, have
i	yh	nymph, it, bit
í	e	me, bee, see
j	yeh	yes, yet
k	keh	king, cut, close
l	el	lean, lamp, love
ly	yee	you, young
m	em	mean, mom, mop
n	en	name, nap, noble

Agár. Villam Arpadhazi (male), courser and CACIB winner in France, Italy, and Switzerland. Owned by Christophe Carrier, Montverdun, France.

ny	nyeh	nyet
o	ock	sock, frock, origin
ó	owe	own, grow, open
ö	euf	huh, Göethe, further
ő	err	fur, her, were
p	peh	pike, poor, pale
r	erh	river, range, row
s	sh	shoe, sharp, shave
sz	ess	soft, said, sense
t	teh	table, trend, take
ty	tyeh	tune, tube, tubular
u	ugh	good, stood
ú	ooh	two, coo, moo
ü	uuh	Cluny, Clair de Lune
ű	yur	curious, music
v	veh	valid, vapor, vast
z	zeh	zoo, zinc
zs	zjeh	pleasure, treasure, measure

18

Pronunciation in Foreign Words

ch	kh	mechanic
q	kwah	quality
w	vee	vat, viper
x	ex	X-ray, lexicon
y	eye or yeh	nylon, Yonkers

Agár. Vera Arpadhazi (bitch), Hungarian Ch. 1987, and French Ch. 1989. Owned by Christophe Carrier, Montverdun, France.

Komondorok. Owned by Claudie Ducret, Rubrouck, France.

General Alphabetic Listing

ábra	oh-brah	illustration
ábránd	oh-brond	fantasy
ábrándkép	oh-brond-cape	daydream
ácsbárd	otch-board	broadax
adoma	ah-doh-mah	anecdote
affektál	ahf-fek-tall	pose/attitude
agyrém	ah-gyew-raym	phantasm
áhitat	oh-heat-at	devotion
ajándék	eye-awn-dayk	gift
ajánlás	oh-yawn-loss	commendation
ajnároz	eye-know-roz	pet (domestic animal)
ajtónálló	eye-towe-knoll-owe	guard
akar	ah-kahr	wish
akvarell	ahk-vah-rell	watercolor
alabárd	ah-lah-board	halberd
álarcosbál	all-arts-osh-ball	masked ball
áldás	all-dosh	blessing
áldomás	all-do-mosh	toast
áldoz	all-doz	sacrifice
alkimista	ahl-kim-ish-tah	alchemist
alkiraly	ahl-kyh-raw-yee	viceroy
alku	ahl-coo	deal
álnév	all-knave	pen name
ámul	oh-mool	wonder
aranybrokát	ah-rah-nyeh-broke-ott	gold brocade
aranyérem	ah-rah-nyeh-ey-rem	gold medal
aranyláz	ah-rah-nyeh-loz	gold rush
aranypor	ah-rah-nyeh-pour	gold dust
arckép	arts-cape	portrait
átirópapír	oh-tyr-owe-pah-peer	carbon paper
azsúr	ah-djoor	lacework
babaarc	bah-bah-arts	baby face
bajadér	bah-yah-dare	Indian dancing girl (houri)
bajnok	by-knock	champion
bálvány	ball-voh-nyeh	idol
barát	bah-rot	friend

békebíró	bay-keh-bee-rowe	magistrate
békedíj	bay-keh-dee	award
bemondó	beh-mond-owe	master of ceremonies
bendzsó	bend-joe	banjo
betyár	bet-your	highwayman
bíró	bee-rowe	judge
bohóc	boh-hoats	clown
brigandi	bryh-gahn-dyh	brigand
büvész	buuh-vayss	conjurer
cár	tsor	tzar
cárnő	tsor-nuh	tzarina
cégér	tsay-gair	billboard
cigányvajda	tsyh-go-nyeh-vie-dah	gypsy chief
cövek	tsuh-vek	spike
császár	cho-sohr	emperor
császárnő	cho-sohr-nuh	empress
cserkesz	cher-case	boy scout
csibész	chib-ace	urchin
csillan	chill-ahn	sparkle
csók	choke	kiss
dajka	die-kah	nursemaid
dal	dahl	song
daljáték	dahl-yaw-take	musical play
dalköťő	dahl-kuh-tuh	songwriter
damaszt	dah-mahst	damask
darabont	dah-rah-bont	guardsman
diadal	dyh-ah-dahl	victory
dicsfény	ditch-fay-nyeh	glory
diszelgés	dys-el-gaysh	parade
dobos	doh-bosh	drummer
dörög	duh-ruhg	thunder
drámairó	draw-mah-yh-rowe	playwright
dzsem	gem	marmalade
dzsentri	gentry	Hungarian gentry (nobility)
dzsida	djih-dah	lance
dzsidas	djih-dahsh	lancer

ebihal	ebby-hahl	tadpole
ejfél	ey-fail	midnight
ekkö	ache-kuh	gem
elc	ale-ts	jest
elgárda	ale-gore-dah	elite
elnök	ell-nuhk	president
elöhad	ell-uh-had	vanguard
elöjáték	ell-uh-yoh-take	prelude
elörajz	ell-uh-rise	sketch
emberke	ember-keh	little fellow
emlék	em-lake	keepsake
épitész	ape-it-ase	architect
erdész	er-days	forest ranger
eröd	ehr-eud	fort
érvágó	air-voh-gowe	lancet
éteri	ate-eh-ryh	ethereal
fabab	fah-bahb	skittle pin
fafúvók	fah-foo-voak	woodwind
fáklya	folk-yee-ah	torch
fáraó	foh-rah-owe	pharaoh
fecseg	fetch-egg	chatter
fegyver	feh-gyew-vehr	weapon
fejtörö	fey-tuh-ruh	puzzle
félisten	fail-is-ten	demigod
felkapott	fell-kah-pot	fashionable
fellegvár	fell-egg-vor	citadel
fénybogár	fay-nyeh-boh-gore	glowworm
fergeteg	fehr-get-egg	storm
fess	fessh	stylish
festés	fesh-taysh	painting
festö	fesh-tuh	artist
fickó	fits-kowe	lad
ficsúr	fitch-oor	dandy
finnyás	finn-nyeh-oss	dainty
flóta	flow-tah	flute
flörtöl	fluhr-tuhl	flirt
föherceg	fuh-ehr-tsegg	archduke
föhercegnö	fuh-ehr-tsegg-nuh	archduchess

frakk	frakk	tailcoat
garda	gor-dah	bodyguard
gardiroz	guard-yh-roz	chaperone
gavaller	gah-vahl-air	cavalier
gerely	geh-reh-yee	javelin
girland	gear-lahnd	garland
gnom	gnowm	troll
grof	growf	count
grofno	growf-nuh	countess
gunyirat	goonyeh-yh-raht	satire
gunykep	goonyeh-cape	cartoon
gyözö	gyew-uh-zuh	conqueror
habhefer	hahb-hef-air	lily-white
hableany	hahb-lay-ah- nyeh	mermaid
haboru	hoh-bor-ooh	war
hadaprod	hahd-ahp-rowed	cadet
hagyatek	hah-gyew-ah-take	legacy
hajfürt	high-fuurt	ringlet
hajnal	high-nahl	dawn
hajos	high-owsh	sailor
halasz	hah-loss	fisherman
harfa	hoar-fah	harp
hazafi	hah-zah-fyh	patriot
hobort	hoe-bort	caprice
hoditas	hoe-dyh-tosh	conquest
hoember	hoe-emb-ehr	snowman
hofelhö	hoe-fell-huh	snow cloud
holabda	hoe-lahb-dah	snowball
hopehely	hoe-pehe-yee	snowflake
hös	heush	hero/valiant
hösnö	heush-nuh	heroine
hovihar	hoe-vyh-are	snow star
huszar	hoo-sor	hussar
icipici	itsi-pitsi	tiny
idealis	id-eh-ah-lys	ideal
idill	id-ill	idyll
igeret	yh-gay-ret	promise

ijász	yh-yoss	archer
ispán	ish-pawn	bailiff
isternnő	iss-tern-nuh	goddess
jassz	yash-zjeh	hooligan
jegesö	yaeg-eh-shuh	hailstone
jeghegy	yaeg-heh-gyew	iceberg
jegrevü	yaeg-reh-vuuh	ice show
jegveres	yaeg-veh-raysh	hailstorm
jelkep	yell-cape	emblem
jogar	yoh-gahr	scepter
juhász	yoo-hoss	shepherd
jutalmaz	yoo-tahl-mahz	reward
kacer	kats-air	coquette
kaland	kah-lahnd	adventure
kalóz	kah-lowz	pirate
kapitány	kah-pit-awe-nyeh	captain
káplan	kop-lawn	curate
karakán	kah-rah-kawn	daredevil
kincs	kintch	treasure
király	kyh-raw-yee	sovereign
királyne	kyh-raw-yee-nay	queen
kockázat	kots-kaw-zaht	venture
kópe	kow-pay	rascal
korbács	kor-botch	whip
korona	koh-roh-nah	crown
kozák	koh-zawk	cossack
kulcsár	kool-tchore	chief steward
lábazat	law-bah-zaht	pedestal
lakáj	lahk-eye	footman
lakkbör	lahkk-burr	patent leather
láncreakció	lawnts-reh-ahk-tsiowe	chain reaction
langesz	lawn-gase	genius
langvörös	long-vuh-ruhsh	flaming/fiery red
lator	lah-tor	rascal
leány	leh-awe-nyeh	girl
leányka	leh-awe-nyeh-kah	little girl
lovász	loh-vaws	marksman

mágia	maw-gyah	black art
matróz	maht-rowz	mariner
melódia	meh-lowe-dyah	melody
mendemonda	men-deh-mon-dah	rumor
mennykö	men-nyeh-kuh	thunderbolt
mereng	meh-reng	daydream
mestermü	mester-muuh	masterpiece
mez+öor	meh-zuh-uhr	ranger
mútargy	mew-tawr-gyew	work of art
müvész	mew-vays	artist
negédes	neh-gay-desh	demure
nyaklánc	nyeh-ahk-lonts	necklace
nyalóka	nyeh-ah-lowe-kah	lollipop
nyil	nyeh-eel	arrow
óbor	owe-bor	vintage wine
oltalmazó	olt-alma-zowe	protector
oriás	owe-ryh-osh	giant
örvény	urr-vay-nyeh	maelstrom
ovació	oh-vaw-tsy-owe	ovation
pajti	pie-tyh	chum
pálinka	paul-inkah	brandy
palota	pah-loh-tah	mansion
pályadij	paw-yah-dee	prize
pártütö	port-uuh-tuh	rebel
pát	pot	spar
prókátor	pro-caught-or	lawyer
rablö	rahb-luh	bandit
rajkó	rye-kowe	gypsy child
regös	reh-guhsh	minstrel
rejtelem	rey-tel-em	mystery
remete	reh-meh-teh	hermit
rikkancs	ryk-kahnch	newsboy
sablón	shahb-lown	model
sámán	shaw-mawn	shaman
sárarany	shaw-rah-rah-nyeh	gold nugget
sarc	sharts	ransom

sejk	shake	sheik
selyem	sheh-yehm	silk
snapsz	shnaps	brandy
sors	shorsh	fate
srák	shrawk	scamp
süveg	shuuh-vehg	fur cap
szaten	sah-tain	satin
szikra	sick-rah	spark
színész	see-nayss	actor
színésznö	see-nayss-nuh	actress
szobrász	sob-ross	sculptor
tábornagy	tobor-nah-gyew	marshall
tábornok	tobor-knock	general
talány	tahl-awe-nyeh	enigma
tánc	taunts	dance
tejút	teh-yoot	Milky Way
telapó	tey-lah-powe	Jack Frost
tücsök	tuu-cheuk	cricket
tüzvörös	tyuz-vuh-ruhsh	fiery
újhold	ooy-hold	new moon
urfi	oor-fyh	young master
urilány	oory-law-nyeh	young lady
urinö	oory-nuh	lady
ürmös	uur-muhsh	vermouth
üstökös	uush-tuh-kuhsh	comet
vadász	vah-doss	huntsman
vadör	vah-durr	gamekeeper
várkastély	vor-kash-tay-yee	castle
várörség	vor-uhr-shayg	garrison
várur	vo-roor	castle lord
vezér	veh-zayr	leader
vivó	vih-voe	swordsman
zarándok	zah-rawn-dock	pilgrim
zászló	zoss-lowe	banner
zerge	zehr-geh	chamois

Agár. Puppies, Villam & Verbena. Owned by Christophe Carrier, Montverdun, France.

Agár. Newborn male. Owned by Christophe Carrier, who is the sole breeder of Agár dogs in France.

Vizsla (smooth). A future champion puppy, Russet Leather of Chalkhills. Owned by James and Patsy Jones of Brea, California.

Descriptive Adjectives

áldott	all-dot	blissful
alkotó	ahl-koh-toe	creative
álnok	all-knock	perfidious
angyali	ahn-gyew-ah-lyh	angelic
badar	bah-dahr	silly
bájos	baw-yosh	charming
baráti	bah-raw-tyh	friendly
bároi	baw-roh-yh	baronial
bátor	baw-tor	bold
bö	buh	exuberant
boldog	bol-dog	happy
bolond	boh-lond	wacky
bozontos	bo-zon-tosh	shaggy
büvös	buuh-vuhsh	magical
cifra	tsif-rah	gaudy
cseles	cheh-lesh	perky
csendes	chen-desh	quiet
csillogó	chyll-oh-goe	gleaming
csinos	chyn-osh	handsome
csodás	cho-dawsh	wonderful
divatos	dyh-vah-tosh	fashionable
édes	ey-desh	sweet
elbüvölö	el-buh-vuh-luh	glamorous
elbüvölt	el-buh-vuhlt	spellbinder
élénk	ey-laynk	spirited
éles szemü	eylesh sem-ewe	sharp-eyed
elpiruló	el-pyr-ooh-low	blushing
elragadó	el-rah-gah-doe	ravishing
eredeti	ehr-ed-eh-tyh	original
erös	ehr-eush	stalwart
erzéklö	air-zayk-luh	sensational

Vizsla (smooth). "My best friends," puppies owned by David Zana-vich, Glendale, California.

farkasszerű	fahr-kash-ser-you	wolfish
fás	faush	woody
fehéren izzó	feh-ey-ren yh-zzow	white-hot
féktelen	fake-teh-len	boisterous
felső	fehl-sheuh	superior
férfias	feyr-fyh-ahsh	manly
fiatal	fyh-aht-ahl	young
forró	fohr-rowe	ebullient
fürge	fyewr-geh	nimble/light-footed
füzes	few-zesh	willowy
gaz	gahz	rascally
gőgös	guh-geush	haughty/aristocratic
gyors	gyew-orsh	quick
halálos	hah-law-losh	lethal
hatalmas	hah-tahl-mahsh	mighty
hencegő	hen-tseh-guh	cocky
híres	hee-resh	renowned
hősi	huh-shyh	heroic
hű	hyew	loyal
huncut	hoon-tsoot	waggish
idősebb	yh-deuh-shebb	senior
ízléses	yhz-lay-shesh	elegant
izom	yh-zom	muscular
játékos	yaw-tay-kosh	playful
jeges	yeg-esh	icy
jó modorú	yowe mow-doh-roo	well-behaved
jól nevelt	yowhl neh-vehlt	well-bred
karcsú	kahr-choo	svelt
kedves	ked-vesh	winsome
kihívó	kyh-yh-vowe	defiant
kimagasló	kym-ah-gash-lowe	outstanding
királyi	kyh-raw-yee-yh	royal
királynoi	kyh-raw-yee-neuyh	queenly
könnyed	kuhn-knee-ed	graceful

Vizsla (smooth). Amer. Ch. Russet Leather Proud Warrior. Owned by Bonnie and Mark Goodwein, Granada Hills, California.

legföbb	leg-fuhb	supreme
lelkes	lel-kesh	soulful
levegös	leh-veh-geush	airy
lovagias	loh-vahg-yash	knightly/chivalrous
mázlis	mawz-lysh	lucky
merész	meh-race	brave
mesebeli	meh-sheh-beh-lyh	legendary
mesteri	mesh-teh-ryh	masterful
mokány	mock-awe-nyeh	spunky
mutatós	mooh-tah-towsh	showy
nemes	neh-mesh	noble
nem felö	nem fay-luh	unafraid
nöies	nuh-yesh	ladylike
nyájas	nyeh-awe-yash	suave
nyugodt	nyeh-oog-odt	sedate

ősi	euh-shyh	ancestral
őszfejü	uhs-feh-yewh	white-headed
óvatos	owe-vah-tosh	discrete
páratlan	paw-raht-lahn	unrivaled
pihés	pyh-eysh	fluffy
pompas	pom-pash	brilliant
ragyogó	rah-gyew-oh-gowe	radiant
rámenős	raw-mehn-uhsh	dashing
remek	reh-meck	scrumptious
rezes	reh-zesh	brassy
rozsdás	rodj-dawsh	rusty
rubintvörös	roo-byn-tvuh-reush	ruby-colored
sugárzó	shoo-gawr-zowe	beaming
szép	sayp	beautiful
szerelmi	seh-rel-myh	amorous
szivós	syh-vosh	tough
társas	taur-shash	gregarious
tintás	tyn-taush	inky
titkos	tyt-kosh	esoteric
törekvő	teur-ek-vuh	aspiring
tudós	too-doesh	scholarly
udvarias	ood-vah-ryh-ahsh	debonair
ugribugri	oogry-boogry	frisky
ügyes	uuh-gyewsh	ingenious
vad	vahd	savage
vajas	vah-yash	buttery
veretlen	veh-ret-lehn	unbeaten
vidám	vyh-dawm	jaunty
vig	vyg	genial/gamesome
villogó	vyl-loh-gowe	flashy
vitéz	vyh-tayz	valiant
vöröses	veuh-reuh-shesh	reddish
zenei	zeh-neh-yh	musical

Komondor. Six-month-old puppy owned by Corrine Trainel, Rubrouck, France.

Komondor. Youngster owned by Corrine Trainel, Rubrouck, France.

Geographic Areas of Interest

Topographical Features

Aggteleg	Ahg-tell-eck	caves
Alföld	Ahl-fuhld	great plains
Bakony	Bah-koh-nyeh	hills
Balaton	Bah-lah-ton	lake
Bukk	Bookk	mountains
Dráva	Draw-vah	Danube tributary on the Yugoslavian border
Duna	Doonah	Danube River
Fennsik	Fenn-shick	plateau
Futó homok	Foot-owe hom-ock	drifting-sands area
Gellért	Guell-airt	hill named in honor of the archbishop
Hortobágy	Horto-baw-gyew	region in great plains
Ipoly (or Ipel)	Yh-poh-yee	Danube tributary on the Czechoslovakian border
Kékes	Kay-kesh	highest mountain peak
Kisaföld	Kish-ah-fuhld	little plain
Körös	Cur-uhsh	river
Mátra	Maw-trah	mountain range
Mecsek	Metch-eck	mountains
Mura	Moo-rah	Dráva tributary originating in Austria
Puszta	Puss-tah	vast arid region
Sárviz	Shawr-vyz	river
Sió	Shyh-owe	canal
Tihany	Tyh-ah-nyeh	penninsula
Tisza	Tissa	Dráva tributary originating in the Carpathian Mountains
Tokay	Tohk-eye	hills known for the famous Tokay wine
Vár	Vawr	hill
Velence	Vehl-en-tse	lake
Verecke	Veh-rets-keh	historic pass in Carpathian Mountains

Fortresses and Battlefields

Esztergom	Ess-ter-gom	fortress
Moháćs	Moh-hawch	also town
Vérmezö	Vair-meh-zuh	known as bloody meadows
Vilagós	Vyh-lah-goesh	battlefield
Visegrád	Vysh-eh-graud	fortress

Vizsla (smooth). Amer. Ch. Russet Leather of Chalkhills. Owned by James and Patsy Jones of Brea, California (pictured with owner at 6 months, 2 days).

Provinces, Counties, and County Capitals

Bács-Kiskun	Bawch-Kish-coon	county
Baranya	Bah-rah-nyeh-ah	county
Békés	Bay-kaysh	county
Békéscsaba	Bay-kaysh-chah-bah	capital of Békés
Borsod-Abaúj-Zemplen	Bohr-shod-Aboh-ooy/Zemplain	county
Budapest	Budah-pesht	national and county (Pest) capital

Pumi. Courtesy of the Canadian Kennel Club.

Csongrád	Chon-grawd	county
Dacia	Daw-tsia	province
Debrecen	Deb-reh-tsen	a fortress city and capital of Hajdú-Bihar
Eger	Eh-gehr	capital of Heves; river of same name
Fejér	Fey-air	county
Györ	Gyew-urr	capital of Györ-Sopron
Györ-Sopron	Gyew-urr-Shop-ron	county
Hajdú-Bihar	Hi-doo-Byh-are	county
Heves	Heh-vesh	county; river of same name
Hódmezővásárhely	Hoed-meh-zuh-vaugh-shauhr-heh-yee	capital of Csongrád
Kaposvár	Kah-posh-vauhr	capital of Somogy; hills of same name
Kecskemét	Ketch-keh-mate	capital of Bács-Kiskun
Komárom	Koh-maw-rom	county
Miskolc	Mish-kolts	capital of Borsod-Abaúj/Zemplén
Nógrád	Know-grawd	county
Nyiregyháza	Nyeh-yh-reh-gyew-hoh-zah	capital of Szabolcs-Szatmár
Pannonia	Pannonia	province also known as Old Hungary
Pécs	Paych	capital of Baranya
Pest	Pesht	county
Salgótarján	Shall-gowe-tahr-yawn	capital of Nógrád
Somogy	Shoh-moh-gyew	county; hills of same name
Szabolcs-Szatmár	Sah-bolch-Saht-mawr	county
Székesfehérvár	Say-kesh-feh-hair-vauhr	capital of Fejér
Szekszard	Seck-sard	capital of Tolna
Szolnok	Sol-knock	county and capital
Szombathely	Som-baht-heh-yee	capital of Vas
Tatabánya	Tah-tah-boh-nyeh-ah	coal-mining center capital of Komárom

Tolna	Tall-nah	county
Vas	Vahsh	county
Veszprém	Vess-praym	county and capital
Zala	Zah-lah	county; river of same name
Zalaegerszeg	Zah-lah-eger-seg	capital of Zala

Commercial Specialty Centers

Badacsony	Bahd-ahch-oh-nyeh	grape-growing center
Halas	Hah-lahsh	lace-making center
Herend	Herend	porcelain-making center
Kalocsa	Kah-loh-chah	center for embroideries
Kócs	Kowch	village where the first riding coaches were built— hence, the word *coach*
Mako	Mah-kowe	onion-growing center
Mezőkövesd	Mez-uh-keuv-eshd	center of the special Matyo embroidery
Mezőkút	Mez-uh-koot	center famous for hand-decorated jugs

Other Points of Interest

Ajka	Eye-kah	town
Érd	Aird	old Budapest town
Ferihegy	Ferry-heh-gyew	airport
Gyula	Gyou-lah	town
Hatvan	Haht-vahn	town
Karcag	Kahr-tsahg	town
Keszthely	Kest-heh-yee	hot springs
Óbuda	Owe-budah	old Budah, also known as Aquincum during second-century Roman occupation
Ozd	Owzd	city
Parád	Pah-rawd	resort
Polgárdi	Pohl-gawr-dyh	town
Répcelak	Rape-tsel-ahk	town
Sárospatok	Shore-osh-pah-tock	castle town, oldest center of education
Tolcsva	Tolch-vah	village
Várpalota	Vawr-pah-loh-tah	city

39

Kuvasz. French Ch. Szentmihaly-Gyongye Fatima (bitch). Owned by
Nicole Thillier, Huisseau sur Cosson, France.

Specialized Listings

Hungarian Rulers

Rulers during the first thousand years of Hungarian history had great impact on the tribal formation and integration to produce today's country as we know it.

Arpad the Conqueror, 890—founded first dynasty
Levente—son of Arpad
Geza I—great grandson of Arpad, embraced Christianity in 973
Stephen I (Saint), 969-1038—completed Christianization of Hungary
Kalman, 1095-1119—most effective of rulers
Bela III, 1172-1196
Endre II—formed the "Magna Carta" of Hungary, an edict known as the "Golden Bull"
Bela IV, 1206-1270—last ruler of Arpad line, son of Endre II
Kun Laszlo, 1272-1290
Endre III, d. 1301—death ended Arpad succession
Stephen V—daughter married Charles of Naples
Robert of Anjou, 1307-1342—known as the first great king, minted the first gold coins; became Charles I, first of the Angevin line
Nagy Lajos, 1342-1382—known as the second-greatest king
Sigismund (Zsigmond), 1378-1437
Albert, d. 1439—founded the Habsburg Dynasty
Ulaszlo I, II, III, 1440-1444—founded the Jagiello line, also ruled Lithuania and Poland
Ulaszlo V, 1442-1452—founded the House of Anjou
Matyas Corvinus, 1458-1490—called "The Just"
Louis II—son of Ulaszlo II; his death heralded the Ottoman domination
Zapolya (John I), 1525-1540
John II—son of John I
Leopold I

A succession of premieres followed. The Habsburgs regained rule of Hungary's western and northern areas after 1526.

Rakoczi I, II—clan ruled Transylvania for thirty years
Karoly III, d. 1740
Maria Theresa, 1740-1780—first woman ruler of Hungary and Holy Roman Empire

Joseph II, 1780–1795—son of Maria Theresa and Holy Roman Emperor
Leopold II, 1790–1792—brother of Joseph II and Holy Roman Emperor
Frances II, 1792–1835—son of Leopold II and Holy Roman Emperor
During the first thousand years, there was no specific standard for succession, and several monarchs ruled other countries as well under different sovereign names and numerical affixes. This is the reason for inconsistency of numerical affixes of Hungarian rulers.

Hungarians Who Influenced History and Culture

Acsady—historian
Aczil—premier
Ady—founder of modern Hungarian poetry
Anda—pianist
Andrassy—count
Balazo—concert pianist
Balog—bacteriologist
Banffy—liberal statesman
Banfi—ecclesiastical scholar
Banky—silent screen star
Bartok—folk-song writer
Bathory—Transylvanian prince, champion of Christianity
Bekassy—actor
Bekeesy—Hungarian-born American physicist
Bernath—artist
Blathy—inventor
Bohem—dramatist
Borbandi—premier
Corvina—famous book illustrator
Csok—painter
Csokonoi—poet
Csoma—researcher of ethnic origins
Cukor—film director
Czinege—minister of defense
Czuczor—poet and linguist
Deak—historian
Dohnanyi—composer
Dorati—conductor
Dozsa—nobleman
Eotvos—baron, minister of education

Esterhazy—princes
Fabri—artist
Faluvezi—premier
Farkas—writer
Feleky—builder of library
Ferber—novelist
Haraszthy—wine merchant
Harmati—Pulitzer prize for symphonic poetry
Heltai—historian
Hetenyi—minister of finance
Horthy de Nagybanya—regent governor
Horvath (Doctor)—minister of interior
Hubay—composer
Illyes—poet laureate
Irion—piano virtuoso
Irinyi—renowned attorney
Jekai—prose poet
Josika—patriotic poet
Karasz—illustrator of children's books
Karolyi—president of Hungarian republic
Keleti—actress
Kisfaludi brothers—founded Magyar stage
Kodaly—composer
Kolcsey—wrote national anthem
Kossuth—led war of independence, national idol
Kukellei—author
Lamberg—count, commander in chief
Laza—premier
Lehar—composer
Lengyel—playwright
Liszt—composer
Loew—newspaperman
Lucas—actor
Lugosi—actor
Madach—dramatist
Marjai—premier
Markoja (Doctor)—minister of justice
Massey—actress
Medgyessy—sculptor

Kuvasz. "Guarding her master's child." French Ch. Szentmihaly-Gyongye Fatima (bitch). Owned by Nicole Thillier, Huisseau sur Cosson, France.

Metternich—minister of foreign affairs
Ocskay—brigadier
Pazmany—revolutionary, enhanced Hungarian language
Perczel—general
Petofi—revolutionary poet
Pozsgay—minister of culture
Puja—minister of foreign affairs
Reiner—conductor
Rejto—cellist
Ripple-Ronai—painter
Rudnay—artist
Solti—conductor
Steuben—baron, glassworks
Szalay—graphic artist
Szechenyi—known as the greatest Hungarian
Szell—conductor
Szent-Gyorgyi—biochemist
Szigeti—Hungarian-born American violinist
Szilard—Hungarian-born physicist
Szonyi—artist
Thokoly—advocated Protestantism
Tisza—prime minister
Usfalvy—scholar
Varga—art editor
Veress—minister of trade
Wesselenyi—baron
Zapolya—magnate
Zita—princess
Zrinyi—count, epic poet
Zsiros—organ virtuoso

Masculine Names of Interest

Andor	Ahn-dor	Andrew
Balázs	Bah-lodge	Blaise
Bandi	Bahndy	Andy
Béla	Bay-lah	(no translation)
Borisz	Bor-iss	Boris
Dönci	Duhn-tsy	diminutive of Ödön
Dusi	Doo-shyh	Ed, Ted
Egyed	Eh-gyewd	Giles

Kopó. Photo from Hungary.

Elek	Eh-leck	Alexis, Alex
Ernő	Ehr-nuh	Ernest
Ferkó	Fehr-kowe	Frank
Gabi	Gah-byh	Gabe
Gábor	Gaw-bor	Gabriel
Gellért	Guell-airt	Gerald
Gergely	Gehr-geh-yee	Gregory
Gerö	Gehr-uh	Greg
Géza	Gay-zah	(no translation)
Guzti	Gooz-tyh	Gus
Gyözö	Gyew-uh-zuh	Victor
Gyuri	Gyoo-ryh	George
Henrick	Hen-rick	Henry
Imre	Ym-reh	Emory
István	Yst-vawn	Stephen
Jancsi	Yahn-chy	Johnny
János	Yawn-osh	John
Jenci	Yen-tsy	Gene
Jenö	Yen-uh	Eugene
Józsi	Yowe-gee	Joe
Karcsi	Kahr-chy	Charley
Károly	Kaw-roh-yee	Charles
Lajos	Lah-yosh	Lewis
László	Laws-lowe	Leslie
Levente	Leh-ven-teh	(no translation)
Lörinc	Luh-rynts	Lawrence
Manó	Mah-nowe	Manuel
Mihály	Myh-haw-yee	Michael
Miklós	Mick-lowsh	Nicholas
Miksa	Mick-shah	Max
Nándi	Nawn-dyh	Ferdie
Nándor	Nawn-dor	Ferdinand
Ödön	Uh-duhn	Edmond
Pál	Paul	Paul
Rezsö	Redj-uh	Rudolph
Samu	Shah-moo	Sam
Samuka	Shah-moo-kah	Sammy
Sándor	Shawn-dor	Alexander
Soma	Shoh-mah	Cornelius
Tibor	Tyh-bor	(no translation)
Tódor	Tow-dor	Theodore

Vazul	Vah-zool	Basil
Vid	Vyd	Guy
Vili	Vyh-lyh	Bill
Zoltán	Zol-tawn	(no translation)

Feminine Names of Interest

Aliz	Ah-liz	Alice
Anikó	Ah-nick-owe	Annie
Aranka	Ah-rahn-kah	Aurelia
Borbála	Bor-baw-lah	Barbara
Dora	Dorah	Dolly
Elza	El-zah	Eliza
Erzsébet	Ehr-djay-bet	Elizabeth
Erzsi	Ehr-gee	Betsy
Fáni	Fawn-yh	Fanni
Gyöngyi	Gyuhn-guiy	Pearl
Hajnalka	Hi-nahl-kah	Aurora
Ildikó	Yl-dyck-owe	(no translation)
Ilka	Yl-kah	Nell
Ilona	Yl-oh-nah	Helen
Janka	Yahn-kah	Jenny
Józsa	Yowe-djah	Josephine
Karola	Kah-roh-lah	Carolyn
Klári	Klaw-ryh	Claire
Magda	Mahg-dah	Maude
Manci	Mahn-tsy	Meg
Margitka	Mahr-gyt-kah	Maggie
Mariska	Mahr-rysh-kah	Polly
Nusi	Noo-shyh	Nancy
Ofelia	Oh-fel-yah	Ophelia
Orsolya	Or-shol-yah	Ursula
Piroska	Pyr-osh-kah	Rosette
Sári	Shaw-ryh	Sadie
Sarolta	Shah-rohl-tah	Charlotte
Terka	Tehr-kah	Tessie
Vica	Vyh-tsah	Eva

The Months

Január	Yah-noo-or	January
Február	Feb-roo-or	February
Március	Mawr-tsy-oos	March
Aprilis	Op-ryll-ysh	April
Május	Maw-yoosh	May
Június	Yooh-nyh-oosh	June
Július	Yooh-lyh-oosh	July
Augusztus	Ah-ooh-goos-toosh	August
Szepyember	Sep-yem-behr	September
Oktober	Ock-taw-behr	October
November	Noh-vem-behr	November
December	Deh-tsem-behr	December

The Days of the Week

Hetfo	Het-foh	Monday
Kedd	Kedd	Tuesday
Szerda	Sehr-dah	Wednesday
Csütörtok	Chuuh-tuhr-tock	Thursday
Péntek	Payn-teck	Friday
Szombat	Som-baht	Saturday
Vasárnap	Vah-shor-nahp	Sunday

Time

felóras	faye-lowe-rawsh	half hour
másodperc	mosh-od-perts	second
negyed óra	neh-gyewd owe-rah	quarter hour
óra	owe-rah	hour
perc	perts	minute

Seasons

nyar	nyeh-ahr	summer
osz	oss	autumn
tavasz	tah-vass	spring
tel	tell	winter

Kuvasz. Head study of French Ch. Szentmihaly-Gyongye Fatima (bitch). Owned by Nicole Thillier, Huisseau sur Cosson, France.

Seasonal Adjectives

nyarias	nyeh -ahr-yh-ahsh	summery
oszi	ossyh	autumnal
tavaszias	tah-vass-yh-ahsh	springlike
telies	tell-yh-esh	wintery

Dances

Csardas	Chahr-dahsh	dances performed by mixed groups, with a variety of steps and formations
Verbunkos	Vehr-boon-kosh	military-type dance performed by men

Cardinal Numbers

egy	eh-gyew	one
kettö	keht-tuh	two
három	haw-rom	three
négy	nay-gyew	four
öt	uht	five
hat	haht	six
hét	hayt	seven
nyolc	nyeh-olts	eight
kilenc	kyh-lents	nine
tiz	tyz	ten
otven	uht-ven	fifty
szaz	sahz	one hundred
ezer	eh-zehr	one thousand

Ordinal Numbers

elsö	ell-suh	first
második	maw-shoh-dyck	second
harmadik	hahr-mah-dyck	third
negyedik	neh-gyew-dyck	fourth
ötödik	uh-tuh-dyck	fifth
hatodik	haht-oh-dyck	sixth
hetedik	heh-teh-dyck	seventh
nyolcadik	nyeh-ohl-tsah-dyck	eighth

Vizsla (wirehaired). Photo from Slovakia.

kilencedik	kyh-len-tseh-dyck	ninth
tizedik	tyz-eh-dyck	tenth
ötvenedik	uht-ven-eh-dyck	fiftieth
szazadik	sah-zah-dyck	one hundredth
ezredik	ehz-reh-dyck	one thousandth

Family Relationships

anya	ah-nyeh-ah	mother
anyós	ah-nyeh-owsh	mother-in-law
após	ah-powsh	father-in-law
edesapa	ey-desh-ah-pah	father
fiu	fyh-yooh	son
fivér	fyh-vair	brother
gyermek	gyewr-meck	child
leany	leh-awe-nyeh	daughter
meny	meh-nyeh	daughter-in-law
nagyanya	nah-gyew-ah-nyeh-ah	grandmother
nagyapa	nah-gyew-apah	grandfather
nagybácsi	nah-gyew-bawe-chy	uncle
nagynéni	nah-gyew-nay-nyh	aunt
nóver	nuh-vair	sister (general term)
unokahúg	oon-oh-kah-hoog	niece
unokaöcs	oon-oh-kah-uhch	nephew
unokatestvér	oon-oh-kah-tesh-tvair	cousin
vö	vuh	son-in-law

Metals and Precious Jewels

acél	ah-tsail	steel
agátkö	ah-got-kuh	agate
arany	ah-rah-nyeh	gold
ametiszt	ah-met-ysst	amethyst
bádog	baw-dog	tin
borostyánkö	bo-rosht-yawn-kuh	amber
egszinkék	aig-syn-cake	ultramarine
ezüst	ehz-uusht	silver
földpát	fuhld-pawt	feldspar

gránátkö	graw-nawt-kuh	garnet
gyémánt	gyew-a-maunt	diamond
gyöngyi	gyuhn-guiy	pearl
higany	hyh-gah-nyeh	quicksilver
jadé	yah-day	jade
jaspiskö	yosh-pysh-kuh	jasper
kristály	krysh-taw-yee	crystal
malahit	mah-lah-hyt	malachite
önötvözet	uhn-uht-vuh-zet	pewter
réz	rayz	copper
smaragd	shmah-rahgd	emerald
szin	syn	cinnabar
vas	vahsh	iron
zafir	zah-fyhr	sapphire

Fruits, Berries, and Herbs

alma	alma	apple
ánizs	oh-nydj	anise
bazsalicom	bah-djahl-yh-tsom	basil
bodza	bod-zah	elderberry
bogyo	bo-gyoh	berry
bors	borsh	pepper
citrancs	tsyt-rahnch	grapefruit
citrom	tsyt-rom	lemon
cseresznye	cheh-ress-nyeh-eh	cherry
eper	eh-pehr	strawberry
fahej	fah-hay	cinnamon
földi szeder	fuhl-dyh seh-dehr	blackberry
gyömber	gyew-uhm-bair	ginger
kakukfü	kahk-ook-fuuh	thyme
kapor	kah-pour	dill
kömeny	kuh-may-nyeh	caraway, cumin
körte	kuhr-teh	pear
málna	mall-nah	raspberry
menta	men-tah	mint
rozmaring	rohz-mah-ring	rosemary
safrány	shaf-raw-nyeh	saffron
szölö	suh-luh	grape
tárkony	tor-koh-nyeh	tarragon
zsálya	soh-yah	sage

Flowers, Trees, and Shrubs

akác	ahk-awts	acacia (tree)
árvácska	or-voch-kah	pansy
babér	bah-bair	laurel
bársony	bohr-shoh-nyeh	amaranth
birsalma	byhr-shall-mah	quince
bodza fa	bod-zah fah	elder (tree)
brácsa	braw-chah	violet
bükköny	buuk-kuh-nyeh	sweet pea
búza virág	booh-zah vyh-rawg	cornflower
cédrus	tsed-roos	cedar
csalán	chal-awn	nettle
erika	eh-ryhk-ah	heather
fagyöngy	fah-gyuhn-gyew	mistletoe
fehér-akác	feh-hair-ahk-awts	locust (tree)
fenyö	fen-yuh	evergreen (tree)
füzfa	fuuhz-fah	willow (tree)
füzfabarka	fuuhz-fah-bark-ah	pussy willow
glicinia	glyh-tsyh-nyh-ah	wisteria
ibolya	yh-bo-yah	violet
irides	yh-ryd-esh	iris
jácint	yaw-tsynt	hyacinth
jázmin	yawz-myn	jasmine
kankalin	kahn-kah-lyn	primrose
köris fa	kurr-ysh fah	ash
levendula	leh-ven-doo-lah	lavender
liliom	lyh-lyh-om	lilly
lonc	lonts	honeysuckle
mak	mahk	poppy
makk	makk	acorn
muskátli	moosh-caught-lyh	geranium
nárcisz	nor-tsyss	narcissus
nyirfa	nyeh-yhr-fah	birch
orgona	or-goh-nah	lilac
öszirózsa	uhss-yh-rowe-zjah	aster
pitypang	pyh-tyeh-pahng	dandelion
rózsa	rowe-zjah	rose
sarkantyú virág	shark-ahn-tyoo vyh-rawg	nasturtium

Puli (brushed). Amer. Ch. Jeffrey's Big Jawn exhibits a beautiful brushed coat. Owned by Lorna E. Spangenberg of Portland, Oregon.

Pulik (brushed). Amer. Ch. Lorwood Bayleaf Pep O'Rika, Amer. Ch. Lorwood Paprika, and Ch. Jeffrey's Big Jawn. Owned by Lorna E. Spangenberg of Portland, Oregon.

sás	shawsh	sedge
selyem pehely	sheh-yehm peh-heh-yee	silk floss (tree)
szegfü	seg-fuuh	carnation
tulipán	too-lyh-pawn	tulip

Birds

bagoly	bah-goh-yee	owl
búbos vöcsök	boo-bosh vuh-cheuk	grebe
csóka	chowe-kah	jackdaw
daru	dah-rooh	crane
erdei szalonka	ehr-deh-yh sah-lon-kah	woodcock
fácán	faw-tsawn	pheasant
fecske	fech-keh	swallow
feketerigó	feh-keh-ter-yh-gowe	blackbird
fogoly	foh-goh-yee	partridge
fülemüle	fuuh-leh-muuh-leh	nightingale
fülesbagody	fuuh-lesh-bah-goh-dyh	eagle owl
fürj	fury	quail
galamb	gah-lahmb	dove
galambasz héja	gah-lahm-bahs heyah	goshawk
gólya	gowe-yah	stork
gúnár	gooh-nawr	gander
harkály	hark-awe-yee	woodpecker
hattyu	haht-tyou	swan
héja	hay-yah	kite
kanári	kahn-awe-ryh	canary
karókatona	kah-rowe-kah-toh-nah	cormorant
királysas	kyh-raw-yee-shahsh	golden eagle
kócsag	kowe-chahg	heron, egret
liba	lyh-bah	goose
ökörszem	uh-kuhr-sem	wren
pacsirta	pah-chyr-tah	lark
pávajérce	paw-vauh-yair-tseh	peahen
pavakakas	paw-vah-kah-kahsh	peacock
pinty	pyn-tyeh	finch

sármány	shore-maw-nyeh	goldfinch
solyom	shoh-yohm	falcon
szalonka	sah-lon-kah	snipe
szarka	sahr-kah	magpie
tengeri sirály	ten-geh-ryh shyh-raw-yee	sea gull
vereb	veh-raib	sparrow

Animals

bocs	botch	bear cub
böleny	buh-lay-nyeh	bison
borz	borz	badger
farkas	fahr-kahsh	wolf
fiatal öz	fyh-ah-tahl uhz	fawn
gödölye	guh-duh-yeh	kid
kekroka	cake-rowe-kah	blue arctic fox
kigyo	kyh-gyoh	snake
kis macska	kysh mahch-kah	kitten
lo	lowe	horse
macska	mahch-kah	cat
majom	my-om	monkey
medve	med-veh	bear
nösteny oroszlan	nuhsh-tay-nyeh oh-ross-lawn	lioness
nösteny tigris	nuhsh-tay-nyeh tyg-ryss	tigress
ocelot parduc	otseh-lot pour-doots	tiger cat
oroszlan	oh-ross-lawn	lion
öszver	uhss-vair	mule
öz	uhz	deer
özbak	uhz-bahk	roe deer
öz suta	uhz shoot-ah	roe doe
rozsomak	rodj-oh-mauk	wolverine
strucc	stroots	ostrich
suta	shoo-tah	doe
szamar	sah-mawr	donkey
tigris	tyg-ryss	tiger
vadaszleopard	vah-daws-leh-oh-poured	cheetah

58

Signs of the Zodiac

Bak	Bahk	Capricorn
Bika	Byh-kah	Taurus
Halak	Hah-lahk	Pices
Ikrek	Yhk-reck	Gemini
Kos	Kosh	Aries
Mérleg	Mare-leg	Libra
Nyilas	Nyeh-yh-lahsh	Sagittarius
Oroszlán	Oh-ross-lawn	Leo
Rák	Rawk	Cancer
Skorpió	Shkor-pyh-owe	Scorpio
Szüz	Suuhz	Virgo
Vizöntö	Vyz-uhn-tuh	Aquarius

Kuvaszok. "The Sentinels." Amer. Ch. Atilla von Liandertal and Amer. Ch. Andrea von Liandertal. Owned by Anna Maria Llewellyn of London, Ohio.

Parts of the Dog.

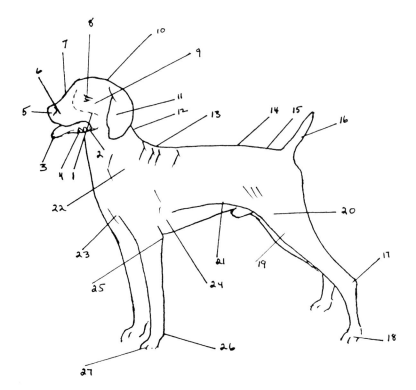

Canine Terminology

Parts of the Dog

1. arc	arts	cheek
2. állkapocs	all-kah-poch	jaw
3. nyelv	nyeh-elv	tongue
4. fog	fog	teeth
5. orr	orr	nose
6. szájkosár	soy-ko-shor	muzzle
7. stop	shtop	stop, break
8. szem	sem	eye
9. álarc	all-arts	mask
10. nyak szirt	nyeh-ahk syrt	occiput
11. ful	full	ear
12. nyak	nyeh-ahk	neck
13. marja	mahr-yah	withers
14. bolthajtás	bolt-hi-tawsh	arch
15. krup	croup	croup
16. farok	fahr-ock	tail
17. zálog	zaw-log	hock
18. mancs	mahnch	paw
19. elfojt	ell-foyt	stifle
20. comb	comb (pronounce b)	thigh
21. feltür	fell-tuur	tuck-up
22. lapocka	lah-pots-kah	shoulder
23. mellkas	mell-kash	chest
24. marhaszegy	mahr-hass-egyew	brisket
25. könyök	kuh-nyeh-uhk	elbow
26. csüd	chyewd	pastern
27. karmok	kahr-mock	claws

Dog Terms

családfa	chal-awed-fah	pedigree
ebadó	eb-ah-doe	dog license
fajkeveredés	fie-keh-ver-ed-eysh	crossbreeding
fajnemesítés	fie-nem-esh-yh-teysh	selective breeding
fajtiszta	fie-tys-tah	purebred
kölyök	kuh-yee-uhk	whelp
kölyök kutya	kuh-yee-uhk coo-tyah	puppy
kutya	coo-tyah	dog (general term)
kutyaadó	coo-tyah-ah-doe	dog tax
kutyabarát	coo-tyah-bahr-aught	dog fancier
kutyafalka	coo-tyah-fahl-kah	pack of hounds
kutyakiállitás	coo-tyah-kyh-all-yh-tawsh	dog show
kutyaól	coo-tyah-ole	dog kennel
kutyatartó	coo-tyah-tahr-toe	dog owner
kutyus	coo-tyoos	doggie
nemző	nem-zuh	sire
szuka	soo-kah	bitch
teliverek	tely-vay-reck	studbook
törzskönyve	turdj-kuh-nyeh-veh	

Types of Dog Coats

átkötött	aught-kuh-tuht	corded
drotszörü	drot-suh-ruuh	wirehaired
göndör	g-uhn-duhr	curly
hosszúszörü	hosh-sooh-suh-ruuh	long coat
vövid szörü	vuh-vyd suh-ruuh	short coat, smooth

Colors in AKC Standards

almás-szürke	almosh-suur-keh	dapple gray
aranyból való	ara-nyeh-bowl vah-low	golden
barna birkabör	bahr-nah byr-kah-buhr	roan
búzából való	boo-zaw-bowl vah-low	wheaten

citrom	tsit-rom	lemon
coboly	tso-bo-yee	sable
csokoládé	cho-koh-law-day	chocolate
csont-szinü	chont-sin-uuh	cream colored
dió	dyh-owe	walnut
ezüst	ehz-uusht	silver
fahéj	fah-hay	cinnamon
farkas-szinü	farkash-sin-uuh	any wolf color
faszén	fah-sane	charcoal
fehér	feh-hair	white
fekete	feh-keh-teh	black
fóka	fow-kah	seal
gesztenye	guess-teh-nyeh-eh	chestnut, tan
gyömbér	gyuhm-bair	ginger
homokos	ho-mock-osh	sandy
homokszinü	ho-mock-sin-uuh	tawny
kakaó	kah-kah-owe	cocoa
kék	cake	blue
kétszersült	kate-sehr-shuult	biscuit
máj	moy	liver
mustár	moose-tore	mustard
méz	maize	honey
mahogóni	mahog-own-yh	mahogany
narancs	nah-rahnch	orange
öszibarack	uh-syh-bah-rahk	peach
özborji	uh-zbor-yee	fawn
paprikajancsi	pap-ryh-kah-yan-chyh	harlequin
pezsgö	pezj-guh	champagne
piros	pyh-rosh	red
platinaszöke	plah-tyn-ah-suh-keh	platinum
rozsda	rozj-dah	rust
sárgabarack	shore-gah-bar-atsk	apricot
sás	shawsh	sedge
szöke	suh-keh	blond
szurke	suur-keh	gray
szürkeség	suur-keh-shayg	grizzle
tarka	tar-kah	pied
tarka kutya	tar-kah coo-tyah	ticked, spotted

63

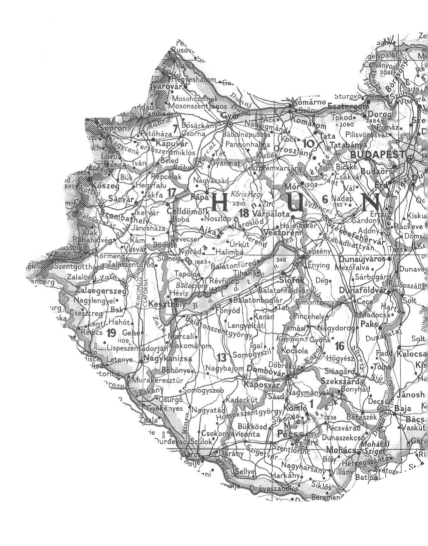